The Cleansing Of Past Defilements

Charles Pretlow

The Cleansing of Past Defilements
December 2024

ISBN 978-1-943412-19-8

Published by
Wilderness Voice Publishing
PO Box 857
Canon City, CO 81215
www.mcgmin.com

"A voice crying in the wilderness –
proclaiming the good news of the coming Kingdom!"

Contents

Defilements Come in Many Ways

There are many ways a person can become defiled in this world. A demon's main job is to defile by implanting internal stains or wounds within a person's soul and inner being (spirit).

Satan and the demonic use wayward and evil people to infect others with harmful-unclean internal beliefs, like a virus. Their sinful words and actions can cause great damage, especially to children.

Children are the devil's primary target, and my years as a counseling pastor, the list of methods used to harm others, especially children are lengthy. Abusive, absentee, dysfunctional parenting along with sexual secret sins in family are a giant part of our national sin sickness.

Our nation's entertainment industry had restrictions and approval ratings. However, over the last sixty years, television, movies, literature, have progressively gained a carte blanche permission to expose the American populace to violence, horror, sexual filth, sorcery, and perversion—exposing the public to all manner of vile and defiling things.

Even in the 1950's we see the progression of defiling movies drawing adults, teens, and youngsters to the Saturday matinees.

Mild and seemingly innocent shows about witchcraft, monster movies, and space creatures grew in great demand at the movies and on television.

Adding to these harmful experiences are the dysfunctional and abusive family systems injecting emotional, mental, physical, and sexual abuse. These harmful secret sins were hidden for years until the 70's and 80's when these abuses began to be made public by brave victims coming forward with their stories.

The 2015 movie Spotlight, a docudrama exposed the extensive child molestations by priests throughout the Catholic church worldwide; the Boston Globe newspaper investigative journalist team (Spotlight) cracked the secret sex abuse by priests in 2001. Of late, other denominations have also been exposed for secret sexual abuse against children.

Childhood sexual abuse is a major reason for mental and emotional problems for children and adult-children victims of childhood abuse.

All forms of defilements stain a child's character growth and often cause duality of character formation (split along the lines of good and evil or dual personalities).

An abusive and dysfunctional home can also form defilements that can wound and damage the child's spirit severely. In the book of James, the tongue is labeled as: *"And the tongue is a fire, a world of unrighteousness. The tongue is set among our members, <u>staining the whole body, setting on fire the entire course of life, and set on fire by hell"</u>* (James 3:6).

The 50s, a Golden Age for America

I grew up in the 50's and was exposed to all manner of unhealthy things, some like those I just described.

One of the most intriguing, seemly harmless, yet scary, was movies about aliens from outer space invading America and the world.

My parents took my brother and I to indoor movies and drive-in motion pictures on a regular basis. Many of the movies during this era were clean and wholesome with a good moral ending.

Frightful Fantasies
become Imagined Reality

However, alien movies were very popular and soaked into our little minds where supposed frightful fantasies became imagined reality. They were very terrifying, infusing the prospect that there was intelligent life on other planets, and will eventually appear to do us harm.

As we became teenagers and young adults, the fear of invasion by aliens from another world faded.

However, the notion that it could happen never completely faded away. Since the 50s this subconscious conviction was reinforced with the production of alien movies that grew exponentially, then coupled with the recent disclosure of government documents on UFO sightings—my guess is that most people in the world, especially in America, believe we are being visited by extraterrestrials. (This includes a multitude of Christians.)

Extraterrestrial Deception

I wrote in one of our recently published books that the second beast in Revelation will most likely appear as an extraterrestrial. This beast will bring fire down from the sky along with other signs and wonders, threatening people with death if one does not worship the first beast (the antichrist).

My contention is that this powerful second beast is a fallen angel released from hell to physically manifest itself, posing as an extraterrestrial. Most of the world, including many Christians will believe this deception.

The world and especially in the American culture most adults, teens, and children have the inner notion that outer space creatures exist, and it is just a matter of time before they present themselves to the world. This conditioning is ever growing.

The Apostle Paul warns: *"The coming of the lawless one is by the activity of Satan with all power and false signs and wonders, and with all wicked deception for those who are perishing; because they refused to love the truth and so be saved. Therefore God sends them a strong delusion, so that they may believe what is false, in order that all may be condemned who did not believe the truth but had pleasure in unrighteousness"* (2 Thessalonians 2:9-12).

Under the Blood in order to be Cleansed

Most Christians, when they first became believers are told everything in the past is under the blood of Jesus Christ, thus all past sins and defilements are forgiven and to be forgotten. However, Scripture in the New Testament clearly instructs all believers to become sanctified (cleansed and transformed) by embracing the discipline of the Lord, and this is possible since we are under the blood of Christ so we can be cleansed and transformed by the Holy Spirit.

Sanctification is a process whereby forgotten defilements, false narratives, false teachings, impurities within the heart, wrong attitudes and hidden bad attitudes, fears, insecurities, pride, self-righteousness, and other leftover old nature issues (that give the devil ground within our inner being) must be brought to our awareness to be cleansed. The Holy Spirit desires to bring these carnal issues to the light to be properly dealt with.

The Apostle Paul instructs Christians to *"Cleanse ourselves from every defilement of body and spirit, bringing holiness to completion in the fear of God"* (2 Corinthians 7:1).

Bad Thoughts & Sinful Heart Felt Desires
The tempter (Satan) will try to ignite issues within the heart and personal spirit by orchestrating a trying situation, a sexually seductive encounter, flattery, or a fleeting thought that ignites more bad thoughts from within. There are many schemes in Satan's arsenal to cause sin and possibly the loss of faith. Satan wanted to sift Peter until he renounced his faith, but Jesus prayed that Peter's faith would not fail.

For the Christian, these hidden issues of the flesh are deceiving and were ingrained within us before we came to Christ. The Apostle Paul lays out another aspect of becoming sanctified in the following passage: *"Put off your old self, which belongs to your former manner of life and is corrupt through deceitful desires, and to*

11

be renewed in the spirit of your minds, and to put on the new self, created after the likeness of God in true righteousness and holiness" (Ephesians 4:22-24).

Catching Our Thoughts

If we are overtaken by any trespass, we have an advocate in Christ to accept our honest repentance and if need be, make restitution. However, the above passage directs us to preemptively deal with our old nature by catching our thoughts before acting upon them. Then we must learn to work with the Lord by having those thoughts that are tied to our "old-self-corrupt-defilements" cleansed by way of renewing our subconscious mind (spirit of our mind).

Now, if a Christian sins deliberately, Scripture is firm on this condition of heart: *"For if we go on sinning deliberately after receiving the knowledge of the truth, there no longer remains a sacrifice for sins, but a fearful expectation of judgment, and a fury of fire that will consume the adversaries"* (Hebrews 10:26-27).

The devil's work is to tempt believers to sin. We may not be sinning deliberately; however, we may easily be overtaken by sin when we still have defilements lodged within our innermost self. Thus, God leads us into the sanctification process.

Again, Peter is a prime example of not recognizing hidden issues within his heart. Peter was definitely sure that he would follow Christ into prison and death.

One of the biggest issues with many believers is unbelief and fear (fear of things in the world and lack fear and trust in God).

The question we need to ask the Lord is: How secure is our relationship with Him?

Be willing to receive an answer by allowing God to test our heart and unconscious mind just as the Scripture states: *"The heart is deceitful above all things, and desperately sick; who can understand it? 'I the LORD search the heart and test the* mind, to give every man according to his ways, according to the fruit of his deeds'" (Jeremiah 17:9-10).

In the book of Job, Elihu conveys how the Lord speaks to us when we are trekking through life thinking all is well. *"For God speaks in one way, and in two, though man does not perceive it. In a dream, in a vision of the night, when deep sleep falls on men, while they slumber on their beds, then he opens the ears of men and terrifies them with warnings, that he may turn man aside from his deed and conceal pride from a man; he keeps back his soul from the pit, his life from perishing by the sword"* (Job 33:14-18).

My Journey With Christ
For myself, when I first became a Christian in 1973 my cognitive belief was that perhaps God did make other beings who live in a galaxy far away. Then back in the mid-80s I began to learn that we can carry past trauma and defilements within our spirit and heart. I was then disciplined

by the Lord to understand that these hidden issues cause trouble and are used by the devil to trip us up.

Soon after that understanding, I gave the Lord permission to show me things within my inmost self that were displeasing to him—things that I may not be aware of but are forgotten and buried deep within.

David, in Psalm 51, after the Lord's prophet confronted him about his affair with a married woman, conceiving a child, and having her husband placed in a certain position during a battle to ensure his death—David writes: *"Behold, you delight in truth in the inward being, and you teach me wisdom in the secret heart"* (Psalm 51:6).

God Cares for Us!

Having this new attitude towards God; desiring him to expose unsavory attitudes, misbeliefs, or unclean issues hidden within my spirit and heart paved for me a wonderful journey.

Through the following years the Lord has shown me hidden issues that proved just how much the Lord loves and cares for me.

Catching fleeting thoughts helped me track down bad attitudes, selfishness, insecurities, and in general loving things of this world more than God. However, many of the harder-deeper wounds and defilements from the past were exposed by dreams that shook my soul. I learned to discern if a dream was from the Lord, my own self, or a devilish counterfeit.

Terrifying Dreams

It was back in 1992 when the Lord revealed to me an unconscious embedded fear through two terrifying dreams in two consecutive nights.

One evening I fell asleep in our rec room on the couch and had a dream where I woke up, yet did not wake up. There was a metallic-like little man standing right by my head. In the dream I became terribly frightened and began to rebuke this strange being in the name of Jesus at least three times, but it would not leave, then I totally woke up.

As I performed my daily duties, I pondered the dream on and off through part of the next day and asked the Lord what it meant but received no insight.

The next night I fell asleep on that same couch in the rec room. Another dream was given to me. In this dream I was standing looking out our glass sliding door and window. In the dream I noticed a glowing ball hovering above the treetops, just floating in no specific direction. Then suddenly this glowing ball zoomed towards me and grew bigger as it got closer. As it became huge it then stopped right in front of me, in our backyard.

The same kind of fear swept over me as was in the first dream the night before. This time I woke up fully feeling disturbed by how frightened I felt and thought of the dream from the previous night.

I knew God was warning me about something, and now he had gotten my full attention. But what are these two scary dreams about? I just could not figure it out.

One thing that did resonate with me was that the last dream reminded me of how the good witch in the movie Wizard of Oz appeared in the movie—in a glowing ball coming closer and larger eventually conveying the good witch of the north.

Hearing God's Voice for the Answer
"And after the fire the sound of a low whisper" (1 Kings 19:12).

Many Christians are familiar with the teaching that one can hear the voice of God filtered through their spirit into one's mind. It is often referred to as a "*still small voice.*" In the English Standard Version these words are translated as "*a low whisper.*"

At the peak of my frustration in trying to interpret these dreams and getting nowhere, I resigned from my efforts and with a sigh of my heart I said, "Lord, I don't get it," then quietly listened.

Witches and Extraterrestrials

Then in a whisper I heard the Lord say, "Son, in your spirit you believe witches and extraterrestrials are more powerful than God."

As an adult Christian, in my conscious mind I would disagree (I feared no one, I'm a former Marine and a strong believer in Christ). However, I knew enough about defilements from the past that can instill unconscious misbeliefs and even hold unbelief and fears that weakens our faith.

In the book of James, the author describes how wrongful words can stain the whole being; harmful words coupled with visions of supernatural activity can really cause damage, especially to young children. Revisiting James: *"And the tongue is a fire, a world of unrighteousness. The tongue is set among our members, staining the whole body, setting on fire the entire course of life, and set on fire by hell"* (James 3:6).

19

In this passage the "entire course of life" in the original language refers to the "wheel of birth" or "cycle of nature." We must understand how powerful outside influences can defile (stain) a child's growing nature. Especially vile or demonic presentations accompanied with visual demonstrations of evil or sin. Satan knows of these stains and uses them against those he defiles even as adults, and many Christians who have yet to be cleansed through the sanctification process.

Invasion of the Saucer Men

Growing up in my family of origin, it was an annual ritual to watch the movie the Wizard of Oz. Witchcraft was its main theme. As I already stated, another frequent venue for our family was going to the movies where quite a few were about extraterrestrials. Then, as kids, we would watch TV shows broadcasting the old fifties science fiction movies.

Knowing that past defilements can affect our inner being and faith in God, I immediately repented of this disclosed inner belief that witches and extraterrestrials were more powerful than God. Then I asked to be forgiven and cleansed from these defilements.

The Wizard of Oz was easy to remember because of the many times I viewed it as a youngster. However, I started thinking about the most terrifying UFO movie I saw

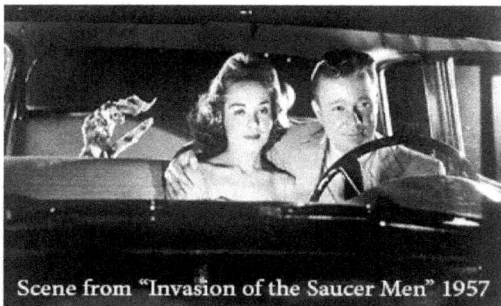

Scene from "Invasion of the Saucer Men" 1957

and remembered one that I watched when I was about thirteen.

"Get me the hell out of here"

This movie was titled "Invasion of the Saucer Men" where the scene showed a severed alien hand having an eyeball on it and could crawl and stab people with long fingernails. In the scene the alien hand crawled into the back seat of a car. In the car were two teenagers, a teenage boy and a girl sitting close to each other in the front seat. That scene had stuck in my mind as a memory for years.

A few days later I was sharing all this with my mother who at the time had finally become a believer in Christ. At the point of sharing with her about the severed alien hand crawling up the back of the front seat of the car with long needles protruding from its fingertips, dripping poison, my mother stopped me.

She interrupted my story and said, "I remember that movie when it first came out. When you were about seven, we all went to the Browns theater in Snohomish to watch that movie, and right at that scene you stood up and said, 'Get me the hell out of here.' Then you walked over to the main aisle and up to exit and of course we had to leave."

Satan Attacks Childhood Faith

Childhood defilements and trauma stain our personal spirit and create damaged emotions (fear, and anger that turns to rage, jealousy, hate, and unbelief in God, the list can go on). In some case our personal spirit can be defiled and wounded, even mangled, that is crushed into pieces and deeply wounded.

"A gentle tongue is a tree of life, but perverseness in it breaks the spirit" (Proverbs 15:4).

"A glad heart makes a cheerful face, but by sorrow of heart the spirit is crushed" (Proverbs 15:13).

"A joyful heart is good medicine, but a crushed spirit dries up the bones" (Proverbs 17:22).

Here are Christ's words about abuse and neglect towards children: *"Truly, I say to you, unless you turn and become like children, you will never enter the kingdom of heaven. Whoever humbles himself like this child is the greatest in the kingdom of heaven. Whoever receives one such child in my name receives me, but whoever causes one of these little ones who believe in me to sin, it would be better for him to have a great millstone fastened around his neck and to be drowned in the depth of the sea"* (Matthew 18:3-6).

Satan's work is to incite people to use their tongue or portray evil to cause defilements that leads to sin. His favorite targets are children in an effort to damage and defile a child's spirit and destroy their childlike faith.

America—A Perverse Culture
Looking back on the American history, we see a trend of cultural perversion and portrayals of evil soaking the masses through entertainment, movies, literature, TV, organized crime, alcohol, drugs, and especially sexuality. These vile and defiling

influences filter down into the secret lives within a multitude of family systems.

As the decades rolled by, God and righteousness, along with prayer was publicly ridiculed to where God and prayer was finally removed from school.

In the 50s my exposure to the things of God and Christ was partly due to my parents. Though they never went to church, they did (as most adults back then) believe in God and the Gospel of Christ.

Grade school exposed me to prayer before the start of school, Christmas and Easter programs and I was encouraged by caring teachers. This influence in my early childhood allowed me to respond properly to the evil scene portrayed in the movie, "Invasion of the Saucer Men."

Yet it left an indelible stain on my spirit that Satan could easily use against me. I had an alternate part of my wounded spirit that was terrified of witches and extraterrestrials.

The Lord used two dreams to que up these wounds and defilements that included intense fear, to cleanse and heal my spirit and to strengthen my faith.

Most wounded and defiled Christians suffer from doublemindedness, that is their spirit and soul are divided. The double-minded word in the book of James is not translated properly. The Greek word translation of "double-minded" in James 1:8, is dipsuchos, in its literal sense means "double-souled," like having two independent wills, or split or multiple personalities.

"Submit yourselves therefore to God. Resist the devil, and he will flee from you. Draw near to God, and he will draw near to you. Cleanse your hands, you sinners, and purify your hearts, you double-minded. Be wretched and mourn and weep. Let your laughter be turned to mourning and your joy to gloom. Humble yourselves before the Lord, and he will exalt you" (James 4:7-10).

Submit To God—Whole Heartedly!

During these last days great deception will entrap many defiled, double minded Christians who are ignorant of God's word on sanctification and cleansing. The last days powers of darkness will engulf multitudes of defiled and lukewarm believers into the furnace of affliction and persecution where many will fall away and be left behind and locked out.

Therefore, submit to God and his discipline so that he can lead you into the true sanctification process—while there is still time.

About the Cover

The cover depicts the demonic influences upon a person. The main tool that Satan and his fallen angels and demons use is other people spewing wrong words that are defiling.

I shared in this publication that the book of James describes the power of the tongue, how it can stain the whole being and start the development of bad character within the hearer, giving place for hell "the demonic" to incite, influence and if possible, allow demons to reside within a person's spirit.

"And the tongue is a fire, a world of unrighteousness. The tongue is set among our members, staining the whole body, setting on fire the entire course of life, and set on fire by hell" (James 3:6).

Jesus taught that these defiling things that people say and do come from within, out of the heart. It is these things that defile not only the person speaking or acting out sinful behavior, but also people who are exposed to these things.

"But what comes out of the mouth proceeds from the heart, and this defiles a person. For out of the heart come evil thoughts, murder, adultery, sexual immorality, theft, false witness, slander. These are what defile a person. But to eat with unwashed hands does not defile anyone." (Matthew 15:18-20).

Hell depends on the sinful and defiled human heart mouthing defiling words and doing evil. This perpetuates Satan's work in trying to destroy faith in God, righteousness, and godly inspired love.

Contact Information

Contacting the author:

Mail: MC Global Ministries
Charles Pretlow
PO Box 857,
Canon City, CO 81215
Phone: (719) 285-8542
Email: charlespretlow@gmail.com
Website: www.mcgmin.com

If this message helps, please consider helping us: Your donations to support this work are most appreciated: Donate today by mail or online by using our secure website with the above contact information. Thank you!

Guest Speaker

Charles is available as a guest speaker. His extensive background in ministry, counseling, and end-of-this-age issues provides sound instruction on overcoming the last-days troubles and wounds to the personal spirit and damaged emotions.

More About the Author

Pastor Charles Pretlow began his ministerial work in 1974, and shares insights gained from years of study, ministry, and counseling Christians who struggled in their walk with Christ. He shares sound teachings to help equip the sincere Christian and those in leadership to effectively minister in these dark days leading to Christ's return. Charles' theology is practical, founded in years of experience and his own recovery from a wounded spirit and damaged emotions. His training in the discipline of the Lord has taught him to rely—not on himself, but on the Holy Spirit and Christ's leadership.

www.ingramcontent.com/pod-product-compliance
Lightning Source LLC
Chambersburg PA
CBHW051051030426
42339CB00006B/300